SOMETHING SINISTER

Books by Hayan Charara

Poetry
The Alchemist's Diary (2001)
The Sadness of Others (2006)
Inclined to Speak: an anthology of contemporary Arab American poetry (2008)

Children's Literature
The Three Lucys (2016)

SOMETHING SINISTER
HAYAN CHARARA

Carnegie Mellon University Press
Pittsburgh 2016

ACKNOWLEDGMENTS

My thanks to the following journals and anthologies, and their editors, in which the poems in this book originally appeared, sometimes in different form and under different titles:

Artful Dodge: "The Other Side," "The Trees"; *Bat City Review*: "You"; *Callaloo*: "A Story," "Being Muslim," "The Rules"; *Connotation Press*: "The God Experience," "Something Sinister Going On"; *Hanging Loose*: "In Memoriam," "Mother and Daughter," "Once," "Signs," "The Weather"; *Literary Imagination*: "Usage"; *The Massachusetts Review*: "O Mother, O Father," "What Is Mine"; *Michigan Quarterly Review*: "Animals"; *Tongue: A Journal of Writing & Art*: "Why the Weather Matters"; *Perihelion Review*: "O!," "Starved Dogs Eating Snow," "23,627 Miles," "Family Portrait," "In a Perfect World"; *Taos Journal of Poetry & Art*: "Dog," "Man Sleeping in the Interstate"; *Weber: The Contemporary West*: "Narrative"

"Animals" was translated into French by Florence Trocmé for *Siècle 21* and also appeared in *We Begin Here: Poems for Palestine and Lebanon*, edited by Kamal Boullata and Kathy Engel (Interlink Books) and in *Uncommon Core: Contemporary Poems for Learning and Living* (Red Beard Press).

"Animals," "Mother and Daughter," "Something Sinister Going On," "What Is Mine," and "Why the Weather Matters" were translated into Arabic by Mohammad Helmi Rishah for *Kikah Magazine*.

"Being Muslim," "The Other Side," and "The Trees" also appeared in *Banipal*.

"Man Sleeping in the Interstate" also appeared in the *San Antonio Express-News*.

"Mother and Daughter" also appeared in *Narrative* and was translated into French by Jean Migrenne for *Siècle 21*.

"Prayer for the Living" appeared in *Al-Mutanabbi Street Starts Here: Poets and Writers Respond to the March 5, 2007, Bombing of Baghdad's "Street of the Booksellers,"* edited by Beau Beausoleil and Deema Shehabi (PM Press).

"The Rules" appeared in *Meena* both in English and Arabic and was translated by Fady Joudah; it also appeared in *Against Agamemnon: War Poetry*, edited by James Adams (WaterWood Press).

"Signs" also appeared in the San Antonio *Current*.

"What Is Mine" and "Being Muslim" also appeared in *Improbable Worlds: an anthology of Texas and Louisiana Poets*, edited by Martha Serpas (Mutabilis Press).

"Usage" also appeared in the following publications: *Behind the Lines: Poetry, War & Peacemaking* (behindthelinespoetry.blogspot.com); *New Plains Review*; *Inclined to Speak: an anthology of contemporary Arab American poetry*, edited by Hayan Charara (University of Arkansas Press); *Phati'tude Magazine*; and *Poem* (UK).

"You" was also included in the *Alhambra Poetry Calendar 2009*, edited by Shafiq Naz (Alhambra Publishing).

I am grateful to the National Endowment for the Arts with whose support this book was completed.

I would like to thank friends and colleagues at Inprint, the University of Houston, and Our Lady of the Lake University, and everyone who offered their wisdom and good will during the writing of these poems, especially Elmaz Abinader, Hosam Aboul-Ela, Kazim Ali, Alise Alousi, Richard Armstrong, Craig Beaven, Lauren Berry, Sean Bishop, Walid Bitar, Mark Doty, Denise Duhamel, Nick Flynn, Kim Garcia, Douglas Goetsch, Marilyn Hacker, John Harvey, Samuel Hazo, Tony Hoagland, Peter Hyland, Randa Jarrar, Paul Jenkins, Fady Joudah, Loren Kwan, Persis Karim, J. Kastely, Brandon Lamson, Rich Levy, Khaled Mattawa, D.H. Melhem, Philip Metres, Jane Miller, Adele Ne Jame, Marilyn Nelson, Naomi Shihab Nye, Ito Romo, Steven Salaita, Martha Serpas, Glenn Shaheen, Deema K. Shehabi, Vanessa Stauffer, Russel Swensen, and Liz Waldner.

Book design by Jackie Sipe

Library of Congress Control Number 2015945710
ISBN 978-0-88748-605-0
Copyright © 2016 by Hayan Charara

10   9   8   7   6   5   4   3   2

for Rachel, Jonathan, and Aden

CONTENTS

BEING MUSLIM

O father bringing home crates
of apples, bushels of corn,
and skinned rabbits on ice.

O mother boiling lentils in a pot
while he watched fight after fight,
boxers pinned on the ropes

pummeling each other mercilessly.
And hung on the wall where we
ate breakfast an autographed photo

of Muhammad Ali. O father
who worshipped him and with
a clenched fist pretended to be:

Float like a butterfly, sting like a bee.
O you loved being Muslim then.
Even when you drank whiskey.

Even when you knocked down
my mother again and again.
O prayer. O god of sun.

God of moon. Of cows
and of thunder. Of women.
Of bees. Of ants and spiders,

poets and calamity.
God of the pen, of the fig,
of the elephant.

Ta' Ha', Ya Sin, Sad, Qaf.
God of my father, listen:
He prayed, he prayed, five times a day,

and he was mean.

WHAT IS MINE

What we come up
against, what we know,
what we've seen

and heard, is like a tree;
once cut down
into so many boards,

or mulched, or burned,
it's no longer a tree—
it becomes a house,

a table, or paper,
or firewood.
It's like that—

to know something
is for it to become
something else.

.

When I was a boy
my mother bought me
new clothes

even as the bills
piled up and the car
broke down.

She saved and sacrificed
for all those shoes,
and shirts, and slacks.

She loved us like
a piece of fruit loves
to be eaten.

•

Years after she died,
I found out
she was arrested

for shoplifting.
I wondered then
about my father's rage,

which came on
like a fever, and how
he must have begged her

to stop, and people knowing,
and talking, and the shame
of it all, how like hunger

it always returned
every time I ruined
a shirt with a stain

or scuffed a pair of shoes
or grew an inch.
My mother was a thief.

I didn't know that
about her. But now
I do. With experience,

it's like this—
once it's yours,
there's no giving it back.

ANIMALS

The phone call, from my wife.
She's hungry, she's pregnant,
someone kicked her

in the stomach—we have to.
I say yes, but the reply
I keep to myself is,

We don't have to do a goddamn thing.
A dog. I'm talking about a dog
I would have otherwise left to starve.

Now though, five years since,
I love this animal, Lucy,
more than I can most people.

•

A boy names his dog and five cats
after our Lucy. The boy, my brother,
born in Henry Ford's hometown,

lives now in Lebanon,
which the Greeks called Phoenicia,
and they tried but failed

to subdue it, same as the Egyptians,
Hittites, Assyrians, Babylonians,
Alexander the Great, Romans, Arabs,

Crusaders, Turks, the British,
the French, the Israelis.
There, my father built a house

with money earned in Detroit—
as a grocer, with social security.
Also there, the first alphabet

14

was created, the first law school built,
the first miracle of Jesus—
water, wine.

.

On the first day
the bombs fall they flee
and the boy asks

to go back for Lucy,
the dog. As for the cats,
No. They take care of themselves.

One week into it
he wonders who feeds them,
who fills the water bowls.

Maybe the neighbors,
the mother thinks out loud.
The father is indignant: *Neighbors—*

what neighbors? They're gone.
The mother is stunned:
What do you mean, gone?

After a month, everyone forgets
or just stops talking about
the animals. During the ceasefire

my father drives south,
a thirty-minute trip that lasts
six hours—wreckage upon wreckage

piled on the roads, on what is left
of the roads. The landscape
entirely gray, so catastrophic

he asks a passerby how far
to his town and is told,
You're in it.

•

My father finds three of the cats,
all perforated, one headless.
The dog is near the carport,

where it hid during lightning storms,
its torso splayed in half
like meat on a slab, its entrails

eaten by other dogs
scavenging on the streets.
Look. They're animals.

Which is to say, there are also people.
And I haven't even begun telling you
what was done to them.

WHY THE WEATHER MATTERS

Above a field in Kansas, or maybe Poland,
light tries but fails to burst through.

Over a mountain range the clouds are fingers reaching
treacherously, or a corkscrew of air, horse manes

or horse tales, or radiating, or fibrous, or iridescent
like a white gem, or undulating.

Across a body of water light's success is luminous.
And jets streaming interrupt the sky, the sky

is interrupted by rumors, and the rumors
never reach the foot of an alpine meadow,

or the waterfront in a city where the tourists
have all gone home, or a fishing dock in a harbor

shaped like nothing at all, or a port or a ship channel,
the shoreline jutting in and out with the appearance

of something man-made, or a hillside anywhere
with hills, or any field with tractors

and telephone poles, railroad crossings, bridges,
street signs, roof lines, and rows and rows

of growth. Below a cloudless sky, there are
no trees, no birds fly past, and inside a house

a man asks a woman, "What's for breakfast?"
and she does not answer. In a valley,

cracks in the earth after the drought.
In another valley, flash floods.

YOU

1
That's right, I'm talking to you,
not him or her.

2
You have been randomly selected
for a security check.

It has nothing to do with you,
your physical features, or your name.

3
Do you now belong
or have you ever belonged

to a radical political organization?
Do you have weapons training?

Have you ever visited a training camp?
Did you pack your own bags?

4
You people send your sons and daughters
on suicide missions.

You animals, you!

5
If you will please step aside.
If you will please remove your shoes.

If you will please come with me.
If you will please leave the premises.

If you will please not harm us.

6
May you live in interesting times.

7
As Americans, you know exactly
what I'm talking about.

As Americans, you may be subject to this.
As Americans, you should be worried.

8
Is it you who are to blame?

9
We cannot help you.
There is nothing we can do for you.

10
The agents came looking for you,
at your father's house.

11
They wanted to ask you questions.

12
I heard about you
being suspected,

detained, interrogated,
jailed without charges,

prosecuted with secret evidence,
found not guilty.

There's no sense in you
making a fuss—

they let you go free, didn't they?

13
Once you begin to see you
differently, as separate

from you, wholly other
from you,

then you can become like us.

14
What has history made of you?

15
Let's get to the point:
It was always

like looking in the mirror—
that face is you. I am you.

STARVED DOGS EATING SNOW

In a field without tracks
a pack of starved dogs

eating snow,
all mutts with knobs of spine

and sharp protruding ribs.
I asked the dogs

How did you get here?
Maybe they'd been there

so long
the falling snow gradually

filled up their footprints,
a small triumph

of gravity over the diminishing weight
of their bodies.

They kept to their feeding
as if snow were chickens

and I could not tell
any difference

between a salivating dog
or a dog with melted snow

dripping from its muzzle.
In the morning I was grateful

the dogs in the dream
did not bark,

bite, or look up.
The day before, coming home,

I drove past
a dog lying on its stomach

in the middle of the road
gasping for air, and from its mouth

gurgled the white foam
of thirst mixed with red.

Unease argued
in my gut over the dignity

of a dog and if it were mine
what would I do and shouldn't

the man or woman who ran over
the dog and not me

be asking these questions?
A while later I drove back

but someone by then
had carried the dog to the curb

and covered it with a towel.
The flies and fleas

were eager. It was summer,
muggy and hot.

23,627 MILES

The note the fifth graders carried
home their teacher did not
think twice about.

Your parents must know
what you've done.

They cheated

on an exam testing
their knowledge
of the universe—

stars, the solar system,
Jupiter's weight, Black Holes,
comets, $E=mc^2$.

What does a ten-year-old
do with relativity? Or
the concept of infinity,

or a theory of everything?
And if the Big Bang and every
instant since turned out

to be a single everlasting
moment under the sun—
so what?

Was he making of them
an example? Teaching them
a lesson? Yes he was,

and as there was right
there was wrong—
this to a wife, a dog, a lawn

mowed on Saturdays,
a house nearly paid for
he went home sure of,

and in a comfortable chair
he shook his head at the chaos
on the five o'clock news,

which that night and every night
thereafter never mentioned
a father striking a son

across the face for not knowing
the distance between
the earth and moon.

THE TREES

Past the smokestacks looming on the river and the rivers
of restless rush hour traffic, I drove north

to where the roads were unmapped and the trees
did not line up in rows one after the other.

I went to get away and to forget, but as it turned out
I broke a sweat splitting and stacking logs

behind the cabin, and like flickering streetlamps
the upturned leaves droned and what is the sound

of cars and trucks churning uninterrupted down
an interstate if not that of a stream in the woods?

For hours on end I watched ants in their lines
of work and stared at grass twitch.

Bit by bit, I grew tired of the world as it was there
doing everything and nothing all at once

and so decided on a drive around the lake
but backing up, distracted, the radio

interrupting the clamor of cicadas
with rumors of a truce

and the murders preceding it,
I whacked the rear bumper into a sapling,

nearly crushing it. I stepped around the tree,
only knee-high, and ran my thumb along its limbs,

carefully, as if the slightest touch
would cause it to fall apart.

Then I looked up and the trees spoke. *Look here*, they said.
We will outlast you all. We belong here more than you.

PRAYER FOR THE LIVING

Go to the mother,
to the father, to the house
where no trees grow,

to the bedroom, the door
closed, to her fear
and to his fear,

and their shame,
their longing, and to their bodies,
their bodies young,

their bodies separate,
their bodies together.
How far must you

go back? Her womb.
Her child body
and his child body.

Go to first hairs.
To flesh, chests, arms, faces,
buttocks, and stomachs.

There, a wrinkle.
There, color,
nipples, and bellybuttons.

Go to the eyes,
see what she sees
and what he sees.

To the fingertips,
which want what
the eyes have made

their own. Go to want,
to love, to what wants
more than love.

Go to sins.
What are your sins?
Go to where the mother

is not mother, the father
is not father, and kiss her lips,
and kiss his mouth.

Do not be ashamed
or afraid.
The past is a strange land.

Go because you can.
Go because you can
come back.

THE WEATHER

In ancient times a plague of locusts showed up to ruin the crops
and this became holy.

A sea surge not long ago made the trees bow down
and people were reminded of their shame.

A child dreams a cow drops dead on a dusty plain
and a farmer weeps for his children.

The weather on that day was a body floating in a street.
The coming storm was a flock of birds cleaning their feathers.

And a kingfisher hung by its beak always turns to face the wind.

NARRATIVE

Servant to the Noble, Generous One.
They called you Tony.

The neighbor said something,
my mother cried in the kitchen,

you slammed a snow shovel
into his face. Red droplets, ice.

After my mother died you began to pray.

I don't remember the first time
it happened. I remember

my sister, her head cracked
against the cinder block wall.

You loved us.

After breakfast you locked her in the upstairs bathroom,
and me in the basement cellar, which had no windows,
and the light bulb you unscrewed.
When you let us out the streetlamps were glowing.

You belted us for laughing.
I could not stop laughing.

"Get the get out of here." "Pick up your mind."
"We are not like the American custom."

Your fifth grade teacher broke
your knuckles with a stick.

Barefoot, knee-deep in snow, me, my mother,
the heavy door slammed before our eyes, I begged
her to go across the street, she didn't dare,
my sister still inside, alone, with you,
we pressed our faces against the windowpane,

we waited and waited, during the snowstorm
nineteen inches fell, it was cold, it was beautiful.

In the morning on the floor, my mother's eyes fluttering.
The coffee cup spilled. The rug stained.

"Please." "Faster." "Hurry."
The ambulance driver apologized.

An aneurysm. A grenade
that ripped apart her brain.

She was happy.

You prayed for a year.
You eat too much salt.

High blood pressure, hypertension, anxiety attacks,
dizzy spells, psychosis, borderline personality disorder.

The argument over the price of eggs.
We cooked you breakfast.

We always returned.

She had stolen money, you found it missing, she denied it,
she was listening to the radio, she didn't hear you
open the door, she saw you, a split second, she tried
to run, you grabbed her collar, you in her bedroom, you
heaved her against the wall, like the first time, she was
a woman now, you were a man each time, you
duct-taped her wrists, she screaming, you bound her feet,
Say you took the money, she wouldn't, you doused her hair
with lighter fluid, the rug soaked, her sweatshirt and jeans
drenched, you clicked the lighter three times, *Say you stole from me,*
Say you stole from me, I swear I will burn you to death,

Okay, Okay, Okay, she said, you threw the lighter at her feet,
you told her, *Do it yourself.*

"Don't worry. I didn't feel
any pain."

"so I just sat there.
then I saw the spider making a web
across a window.
I found a match, walked over,
lit it and burned the spider to
death.
then I felt better.
much better."

Lopressor, Vasotec, Aldomet, Loniten, Inderal, Zoloft,
Paxil, Klonopin, Valium, Norpramin, Lithium, Xanax,
Lamictal, Tegretol, Desyrel, Prozac, Effexor.

You broke the neighbor's nose.
A bloody towel.

Ice.
Water.
0.9% salt.

Sodium chloride, potassium chloride, calcium chloride,
sodium bicarbonate, diarrhea, vomiting, cold sweats.

Lamb brains
fried in butter with garlic and salt.

The gun on the counter.
I aimed at the moon.

We always returned.
Please, stop.

You loved us. You remember. You forget.

I ran past the bar on the corner, the burned-out diner,
the liquor store, the bowling alley, the church,
the high school, the donut shop, the deli, the park,
the baseball diamond, the fence, the hill beside
the railroad tracks, the railroad tracks.

ONCE

Outside, along the streets, traffic moves,
and news of the bombing, over a country

far off, is carried with the wind, and a taxi
honks at an old woman pushing a grocery cart,

and to me, alone in a darkening room,
comes a vision of my mother.

How long, I want to know, how much,
how many times will I stare at people

disappearing into the cold of night,
or lights crossing a bridge, or nothing at all,

and still expect to see her, waiting, for me
to come home, years and years after she died?

At least this once. Hundreds of miles away,
I stand on the porch, the house

surrounded by rustling trees, and inside,
through the living room with the cheap sofas

bought from the Jew who loved bargaining
with the Arabs, and the Arabs loved him

in return, the old floors creak, and at a table
in the kitchen, I sit beside her,

and she does not speak, but against
my slouched back, which again and again

she told me to straighten, and I never did,
I feel her touch. This is no miracle.

This is only a merciless vision.
When I open my eyes, there is no one

beside me. As suddenly as she was there,
she is gone. And she will never come back.

THE OTHER SIDE

Once tall pines stripped
of branches, the light poles

lean toward where the hurricane
went and there a ship channel,

quarry heaps along its banks,
warehouse stacks, rail yards

rusting and humming,
and the refineries on the shore,

their oil slicked floors iridescent
as a school of fish, and far off

lights on the horizon, and farther,
more lights, and a vanishing,

which is the end of one thing
and the beginning of another.

There my father waits for word
to come, of a ceasefire.

Outside his window over rows
of fig and olive, cedar and sumac,

and a hillside silvered
by a moon looming large above

the sea, and the air salted
by the sea, night descends.

Years he spent telling us
how much he hated living

in the wrong country, and now,
finally back on the other side

of the world, he would be content
except for the storm

still overtaking him.

IN A PERFECT WORLD

A man thinks he is lucky
to smoke cigarettes and not cough.
The car windshield is fogged

and the heater busted, but there is still
a moon to be grateful for.
And it is bitter cold outside

so what's more he slips on
the wool gloves his wife spent
a month knitting, and wears them

for her, believing a simple gesture
can make her happy.
One night he takes the long way home,

and for a long time he does not speak,
and standing on the front porch
he takes a deep breath,

and through the window he eyes
a plate of rice and a glass of milk
on the table, and a pot of beans

and a greasy frying pan
on the stove. He can hear his wife
humming the same music

he tried but failed all day
to rid from his head.
There is a word for what he does,

a simple word, and the word
moves through the world,
and its melody is silence.

What happiness to know more than
the known world, to believe in
what cannot be seen.

What joy to welcome the dead
into our lives.
And what misery.

In a perfect world he knows
which really counts—in a perfect world,
which this is not.

MOTHER AND DAUGHTER

The mother says, I am afraid.
The daughter says, I am afraid.

The mother says, My feet are cold.
The daughter says, My feet are cold.

The mother says, The car is sinking.
The daughter says Yes, the car is sinking.

The mother says, The water is heavy,
and the daughter says, The water is very heavy.

The mother says, I am too young for this.
The daughter says, I want to grow old.

The mother says, I can see the sky,
and the daughter says, I can also see the sky.

How about the moon, the mother says,
and the daughter says, I can see the moon.

What else hurts you, the mother says
and the daughter says, What about you.

I forgot to tell your father something,
the mother says and the daughter says,
I forgot to tell my father something.

The mother says, I do not want to die.
I do not want to die, the daughter says.

I wanted to be a good mother, the mother says.
Sometimes you weren't, the daughter says.

Sometimes you weren't a good daughter either, the mother says
and the daughter says, I wanted to be good.

I can hear my heart, she says.
I can hear my heart, she says.

I wish I loved Jesus, she says and she says,
I wish I loved Jesus.

She says, The thud is unbearable.
She says, The thud is unbearable.

What do you mean you wish
you loved Jesus, she says
and she says, The water is dark.

My clothes are getting heavier, she says.
Heavier, she says, and heavier.

She says, The water is up to my chin now, and she says,
It is up to my chin too.

What if this is the last thing I say to you, she says
and she says, What if this is the last thing I say to you.

She says, I cannot hold on much longer.
Please, she says, hold on longer.

The water is at my mouth, she says,
and she says, Even if it is at your mouth.

THE GOD EXPERIENCE

A scientist in America believes
God is a nerve cell.

All it takes is getting struck by lightning
or bumped hard on the head,

or a lack of oxygen—a near drowning,
a choking—for a man to say,

"God talked to me."
And why not?

Martin Luther turned from the law
to becoming a monk

after a heavenly bolt knocked
him from his horse,

which reminds me, when Mohammed
saw the divine presence

an angel filled the sky
with light and a voice growing

louder and louder came from
every direction, and this

reminds me of a sentence
in a field guide to weather:

"If thunder is the atmosphere's noisiest production,
lightning is its most dazzling."

Having never had the God experience
or anything like it

I was at a loss when sobbing and rambling
my sister called

not a week after the sudden death
of our mother

and said,
"She was in my room."

I didn't ask if she meant
she'd seen her

in a dream or as a ghost.
And I did not bring up

PTSD
or anxiety-induced hallucinations.

I did not have to.
My silence alone provoked her into

saying, "I wasn't dreaming."
And if she had doubts

about God or the afterlife or seeing
our mother again, that night

she believed.
As for me, I was simply jealous.

I loved my mother and let her death
ruin my life, yet she

never showed up, no matter
how much I drank

or smoked or banged my head
against the walls.

I was living in
New York City, a young man

walking the streets most every day
and night, during which

I met dozens of men with whom
God had spoken.

If I had money in my pockets
I gave it to them,

and when they tried talking to me
I walked away.

MAN SLEEPING IN THE INTERSTATE

The headlights caught a glimpse of him and in
that instant he was something other than a man
lying on his side with his knees and arms bent

to shield himself. Because his shirt was either red
or bloody, he was a rusted muffler come to a stop
after breaking off and blazing the road like a meteor;

he was every couch or mattress in the middle
of a lane surprising drivers into swerves and curses
and shutting down highways in places like Tulsa,

Oklahoma; he was the unexpected happening
which happened just the same; and when
I hit him, my stomach sank, and when the tires

rolled over he was only and always just a man,
already dead though, struck first by a taxi now parked
on the shoulder, bumper cracked, hood streaked,

windshield caved in where the head smashed,
and the cabbie, his hands still on the steering wheel,
kept asking, "Was that a man? Was that a man?"

In the backseats there was a galaxy of glass
and a woman on business who answered him,
"Yes, yes, for the last time, yes."

THE RULES

An interruption—
a rally of dark men with dark eyes chanting,

a language that is not translated.
Soldiers grin for a camera,

a flag is raised over the rooftop of a collapsed pharmacy,
and children play board games

in basement shelters.
The Minister of Defense

on learning to kill:
This has happened before.

An old man and woman; an umbrella
protects their heads, and there is no rain—

the umbrella a sign of resistance.
The Majority Leader explains

diplomacy's drawbacks, a vote is taken
to rush aid, a shipment of bombs.

From the rubble a man lifts a girl,
the girl's limbs slip from their sockets—

my father, an old man,
watches the arms leave the body.

A woman in a café speaks loudly.
They deserve it, she says—Should I tell her

I call my father every night?
"Are you alive?" "I'm alive."

I account for the absurd.
Stay calm. Remain quiet.

I know the rules.
They are no longer written in books.

I know what to do
I keep telling myself. I know

what to do.

SIGNS

The sun and moon in the sky together
were a sign. A dog stopped barking

and this warned of heartache:
the hem of a blue dress, the bright

bare feet, the family discovered in a ditch.
A man wonders if the moon

can still be written about.
A long time ago the moon was a mirror.

Men used it to decide marriages, to buy
cattle, to free captives, to dig graves.

A STORY

Some will call the suicide bomber
a coward but seeing him

you think only, *Hungry*,
stumbling as he is toward you,

to the tent where pilgrims
stop to eat and drink.

Behind you a woman in a black robe
scoops rice with her fingers.

Beside her a girl, restless, runs out
onto the dusty two-lane road

that the bomber now crosses.
This is happening

at the end
of forty days of mourning,

the anniversary a martyrdom.
The girl returns breathless

and the mother gives her
a glass of clean water.

You watch the ripple down
her throat, and out of sunlight

the man approaches—
his eyes, like yours, are brown.

Now you hear someone say, *Sit, sit*.
It is the mother talking to the daughter.

And now someone is shouting,
and now there is the terrible noise.

Every person is a story.
You are the man who walked out

as he walked in, the bomb went off,
and you lived to tell.

IN MEMORIAM

A man says *America makes everything easy,*
except life.

Under the circumstances, I don't dare complain.

Overheard: All through the drive, twenty hours to Disney World,
We've got it good and *We've got it made.*

Unspoken: lower back pain, a slipped disc, insomnia of the anxious,
habits let loose by ancient habits.

Who can disagree with a man who wanted to die happy
though he was miserable his whole life?

Thin in his suit my uncle who has not worked
since 1976 and his wife dying of emphysema,

they, seated side by side, come for the neighbor
who during the afternoon shift at the factory

was telling jokes about the Polacks
when an engine block slipped from its harness and crushed his brain.

Eventually everyone departs a wife says,
and a husband nods *Yes.*

Every story like this: you are here, then you are gone.

Behind a hill off the interstate—my mother's grave,
which I last saw a very long time ago.

It is easier that way, then
it is harder.

FAMILY PORTRAIT

A bad haircut
is the father's anger,
his dark hair and eyes

darker like night
falling on a furious crowd.
He stares straight

ahead and the future
looks back and it recognizes
the tie he wore at

his wife's funeral,
which he will relive
again and again.

At the end she was
unhappy but in the end,
because the future

depends upon the past,
she is a beautiful
young mother now

and her large eyes
remain open on the cold
morning she collapses

and the stain is
a long time forgetting.
In the photograph,

the daughter doesn't yet
know her life story,
and she will not tell it.

The son waits
and waits and he will
wait and wait.

If the mother
could see them looking
at her now she would

disapprove. Sorrow
ends only in sorrow,
a person can be

sure of this.
But there is also joy
in being sad.

O MOTHER, O FATHER

There, the '76 Buick Riviera, the young husband
and wife in it, empty coffee cups between them,
a pack of cigarettes, a map, and long uninterrupted silence.

The low but audible AM radio is like the engine
which is like the tires against asphalt which is like
the boy in the backseat humming. There, too, the name

on the radio of the missing girl, eyes blue,
blond hair, wearing eyeglasses, last seen pushing
a lawnmower in Rock Hill, South Carolina,

on the kitchen counter a glass of iced tea left untouched.
The husband asking *What's this world come to?*
is like the mother turning off the radio which is like

both of them counting the miles. There are still
a hundred miles to go and the only noise is the father
clicking the radio back on, and from the back, tugging

the mother's shirtsleeve, the boy asks why,
Why is the girl missing? The mother rolling down
the window is like the father continuing to smoke

is like the son leaning closer and asking again.
And there, on the radio, *foul play suspected*,
and the father's quiet like a mother's hush

which is like calm indifference, and the sun warm
and blinding like the dashed white lines blurred
on the highway like evergreens vanishing into the horizon.

I hear the crackle of the news, the hushed speech up front.
I smell the dank ashtray, the smoke. I see the blue skies
and the trees barely visible vanishing on either side.

Father, I am not like you. I am older than
you were then and you are older than I thought possible.
And mother, you are not like any of us anymore.

You there, always and forever there,
in the termination that obliterates everything else.
O my mother. O my father, what of this world,

which forgives the misdeeds of its children. O world,
you never stopped for anyone. O Eva Gerline Debruhl,
from Rock Hill, South Carolina, you are still missing.

SOMETHING SINISTER GOING ON

I'm one guy sitting in a chair, you're a bunch of guys
on the street, screaming, chanting,
"Death to this" and "Death to that."
You're always so angry.
You should try being calm, letting go, own a pet, quit caffeine.
I don't smoke—maybe you should be more like me.
A person like me enjoys bacon, pork chops, corned beef hash,
eggs over easy, French fries, woodwork, girls in bikinis,
Netflix, instant coupons, running, camping, Coney dogs,
souvenir coffee mugs, cable survivor shows, oak trees, rivers,
the country, family reunions in Corpus Christi,
the Detroit Lions, voting, complaining about voting,
deep-fried Oreo cookies, rodeos, state fairs, baseball,
and apple pie—
I know, I know, how American of me!
It's true.
I could stand to lose five pounds, I can turn off the war,
I can afford to be peaceful.
Did I tell you about my grandfather who died from the same bombs
you are raising your fists at?
You know, my father's piece of sky is in the same time zone
as yours.
Something's happening.
I can feel it—can you feel it?
It's like two drops of water coming together and then the flood,
like seeing through the right eye
and then the left, back and forth, one eye then the other,
a headache, really, if you try.
It is 5:35, outside my window a tree is blossoming.
Maybe this is why I want to compare you with birds.
Except, seeing you I do not think *nightingales*
or *ruby-throated hummingbirds*.
Who ever heard of such a thing, turning grown men into birds?
You're restless like bees—I'm restless, you're restless.
We are one and the same.
We are getting close, at least.
Let me be clear about what is happening:
I'm here, you're there—

The trees are blossoming—
Red birds flash past my window.
I can't help but think of fire.
I see a mob, men holding matches to the trunks of trees,
a row of fire ants marching past.
A burning tree, you know, is like a redhead on fire, except
a tree does not scream
and even trees without leaves survive.
It is midnight, and all the trees are gone.
This is mayhem.
You're making it impossible for me to live.
You want to take this outside?
I didn't think so.
Cowards, the lot of you.
Flying airplanes into buildings.
Bunch of yellowbellies.
My wife says I spend too much time talking to myself.
Oh great.
Now I have become you, and you me.
What are we now if not the birds and the bees in the trees?
Something sinister is going on.
Listen:
A fire speaks to a tree, the flame is patient—
it loves the tree to death.

DOG

I drove past a dog mangled
in the middle of a busy street,
the asphalt a pillow for its head,

its front paws stretched across
the dashed yellow line
separating one way from another.

I did nothing, not even turn off
the radio, but kept driving,
one more car in an unyielding

noisy procession of cars,
the dog vanishing with the horizon
in the rear view mirror.

And now? Now I think
the traffic poles were trees
and together with the streetlamps

they made a forest blazing
with the silent fires of autumn.
There was so much quiet

the falling leaves were startling
and if the ants and worms
could have spoken

I would have heard them.
Come to think of it
I'm sure I heard the unchanging

music of water, a nearby river
or stream, a sound no different
than the sound of traffic.

And if there was a truck rumbling
across a bridge it was thunder,
and lightning was the flash

of high beams, and a driver
beeping back at another
was an owl making a noise

and another replying.
It's even possible rain was falling
to baptize the animal into

its new life, and now
there's no doubt:
I stopped, I moved the dog,

I stood there a while.
And when the sun burst forth
to astonish everything in sight—

or the moon, either would be fine—
the world whispered, *Now, now,*
you're not alone.

0!

The sun will turn into charcoal,
and the sky a hole where once it shined.

Sons and daughters will become men
and women whose sons and daughters

have children whose children
do not know them. Or something else,

or something worse, or a thing unthinkable.
What can't be imagined? No trees,

which a long time ago touched each other
from continent to continent? Or bees,

which are in the Qur'an and already disappearing?
Or the things done again and done again

and done again, which is sometimes called a life?
All the almost-babies in the bellies of all

the almost-mothers, they will come screaming
into the world and they will go quietly,

so quietly almost every man, woman,
child, and animal will be none the wiser.

Save us from our own black holes.
Save us from Genghis Khan.

Save us from the Bubonic Plague,
from the Dead Sea, from Death Valley,

and the ravages of the moon, which will
one day tumble onto our heads.

Save us from that which keeps
all the good scientists awake so late.

O, one day there will be no more,
"What's up, baby?" No more, "Good night,

Sweetie Pie." No more, "Honey,
take out the trash." No more, no more.

One day everything will be gone.
Everything will be different. One day,

but not today, and not tomorrow,
and not soon at least.

USAGE

An assumption, *a* pejorative, *an* honest language,
an honorable death. In grade school, I refused to *accept*
the mayor's handshake; he smiled at everyone *except*
people with names like mine. I was born here.
I didn't have to *adopt* America, but I *adapted* to it.
You understand: a man must be *averse* to opinions
that have *adverse* impacts on whether he lives
or dies. "Before taking any *advice*, know the language
of those who seek to *advise* you." Certain words
affected me. Sand nigger, I was called. Camel jockey.
What was the *effect*? While I *already* muttered
under my breath, I did so even more. I am not
altogether sure we can *all together* come. Everything
was not *all right*. Everything is not *all right*.
Imagine poetry without *allusions* to Shakespeare,
Greek mythology, the Bible; or *allusions* without
the adjectives "fanatical," "extremist," "Islamic,"
"right," "left," "Christian," "conservative," "liberal."
Language written or translated into a single tongue
gives the *illusion* of tradition. *A lot* of people murder
language—*a lot* fully aware. *Among* all the dead,
choose *between* "us" and "them." *Among* all the names
for the dead—mother, father, brother, sister,
husband, wife, child, friend, colleague, neighbor,
teacher, student, stranger—choose *between*
"citizen" and "terrorist." And poet? *Immoral*,
yes, but never *amoral*? Large *amounts*, the number
between 75 and 90 percent of the estimated
150 million to 1 billion—civilians—killed during wars,
over all of recorded human history. *Anxious* is "worried"
or "apprehensive." American poetry, Americans.
Young, I learned *anyone* born here could become
President. Older, I can point to *any one* of a hundred
reasons why this is a lie. *Anyway*, I don't want to be
President, not of a country, or club, not here or there,
not *anywhere*. He said, "I turned the car around *because*
it began raining bombs." There's no chance of ambiguity—
an *as* here could mean "because" or "when"; it makes

no difference—he saw the sky, felt the ground,
knew what would come next; it matters little
when the heart rate in less than a second jumps from
70 to 200 beats per minute. What they did
to my grandfather was *awful*—its wretchedness,
awe-inspiring; its cruelty, terrible; it was *awfully*
hard to forget. Just after 8:46 AM, I wondered *awhile*
what would happen next. At 9:03 AM, I knew
there was going to be trouble for a *while* to come.
When in her grief the woman said, "We're going
to hurt them *bad*," she meant to say, "We're going
to hurt them *badly*." For seventeen days, during
air strikes, my grandfather slept on a cot *beside*
a kerosene lamp in the basement of his house. *Besides*
a few days worth of pills, and a gallon of water,
he had nothing else to eat or drink. Given these conditions,
none of us were surprised that on the eighteenth day,
he died. *Besides*, he was eighty-two years old.
I can write what I please. I don't need to ask, *May I?*
Like a song: men with *capital* meet in the *Capitol*
in the nation's *capital*. Any disagreements, *censored*;
those making them—poets, dissenters, activists—
censured. The aftermath, approximately 655,000
people killed. "The Human Cost of War in Iraq:
A Mortality Study, 2002-2006," Bloomsburg School
of Public Health, Johns Hopkins University (Baltimore,
Maryland); School of Medicine, Al Mustansiriya University
(Baghdad, Iraq); in cooperation with the Center
for International Studies, Massachusetts Institute
of Technology (Cambridge, Massachusetts).
The figure just *cited*—655,000 dead—resulted from
a household survey conducted at actual *sites*, in Iraq,
not the Pentagon, or White House, or a newsroom,
or someone's imagination. Of *course*, language has been
corrupted. Look, the President, who speaks *coarsely*,
says, "We must stay the *course*." The problem with
"Let your *conscience* be your guide" is you must first
be aware, *conscious*, of the fact that a moral principle

is a subjective thing. I wonder: when one "smokes 'em
out of a hole," if the person doing the smoking
is *conscious* of his *conscience* at work. Am I fully *conscious*
of how I arrived at this? The *continual* dissemination
of similar images and ideas. The *continual* aired footage
of planes striking the towers, the towers crumbling
to the streets, dust, screams, a *continuous* reel of destruction,
fear, as if the attacks were happening twenty-four hours
a day, every day, any time. For a while, I *couldn't care less*
about war. Then I saw corpses, of boys, who looked
just like me. This was 1982, at age ten. Ever since,
I *couldn't care less* why anyone would want it.
In 1982, any one of those boys *could have* been me.
Now, it's any one of those dead men could be me.
The Secretary of State offered such *counsel*
to the ambassadors of the world that the United Nations
Security *Council* nodded in favor of war. *Criterion*
easily becomes *criteria*. Even easier: to no longer
require either. The *data* turned out false. The doctrine
of preemption ultimately negated its need. While we
both speak English, our languages are so *different from*
each other, yours might as well be Greek to me.
When the black man in the park asked, "Are you
Mexican, Puerto Rican, or are you Pakistani?"
and I said, "I'm Arab," and he replied, "Damn.
Someone *don't* like you very much," I understood
perfectly what he meant. The President alluded
to the Crusades because of (not *due to*) a lack
of knowledge. Later, he retracted the statement,
worried it might offend the Middle East;
it never occurred to him the offense taken was *due to*
the bombs shredding them to bits and pieces. "You are
either with us or with the terrorists" (September 20, 2001).
"You're *either* with us or against us" (November 6, 2001).
The day after, the disc jockey advocated, on air,
a thirty-three cent solution (the cost of a bullet)
to the problem of terrorists in our midst—he meant
in New York; also, by terrorists, I wonder, did he know

he meant cab drivers, hot dog vendors, students, bankers,
neighbors, passersby, New Yorkers, Americans;
did he know he also meant Sikhs, Hindus, Iranians,
Africans, Asians; did he know, too, he meant Christians,
Jews, Buddhists, Atheists; did he realize he was *eliciting*
a violent response, on the radio, in the afternoon?
Among those who did not find the remark at all *illicit*:
the owners of the radio station, the FCC, the mayor,
the governor, members of the House, the Senate,
the President of the United States. *Emigrate* is better
than *immigrate*. Proof: no such thing as illegal *emigration*.
Further proof: emigration is never an election issue.
I heard *enthusiastic* speeches. They hate our freedoms,
our way of life, our this, that, and the other, *and so on*
(not etc). Not *everyone* agreed *every one* not "with us"
was "against us." Detroit was *farther* from home
than my father ever imagined. He convinced himself
soon after arriving here he had ventured *further*
than he should have. *Fewer* people live in his hometown
than when he left, in 1966. The number, even *less*,
following thirty-four straight days of aerial bombardment.
First (not *firstly*) my father spoke Arabic; *second*
(not *secondly*) he spoke broken English; *third* (not *thirdly*)
he spoke Arabic at home and English at work;
fourth (not *fourthly*) he refused to speak English
anymore. Not every poem is *good*. Not every poem
does well. Not every poem is *well*, either. Nor does
every poem do *good*. "To grow the economy"
is more than jargon. Can a democracy *grow*
without violence? Ours didn't. They still plan to *grow*
tomatoes this year, despite what was done.
Several men, civilian workers, identified as enemies,
were *hanged* on a bridge, bodies torched, corpses
swaying in the breeze. Photographs of the dead
were *hung* with care. I can *hardly* describe what is
going on. Day after day, he told *himself*, "I am
an American. I eat apple pie. I watch baseball.
I speak American English. I read American poetry.

I was born in Detroit, a city as American as it gets.
I vote. I work. I pay taxes, too many taxes. I own a car.
I make mortgage payments. I am not hungry. I worry
less than the rest of the world. I could stand to lose
a few pounds. I eat several types of cuisine
on a regular basis. I flush toilets. I let the faucet drip.
I have central air conditioning. I will never starve
to death or experience famine. I will never die
of malaria. I can say whatever the fuck I please."
Even words succumbed; *hopefully* turned into
a kind of joke; *hopeful*, a slur. *However*, I use the words,
but less, with more care. The President *implied*
compassion; but *inferred* otherwise. This is not
meant to be *ingenious*. Nor is it *ingenuous*.
The more he got *into* it, the more he saw poetry,
like language, was *in* a constant state of becoming.
Regardless, or because of this, he welcomed the misuse
of language. Language is *its* own worst enemy—
it's the snake devouring *its* own tail. They thought
of us not *kind of* or *sort of* but as *somewhat* American.
Lie: "To recline or rest on a surface?" No. "To put
or place something?" No. Depleted uranium, heavy
like *lead*; its use—uranium shells—*led* to birth defects.
When in his anger the man said, "We're going
to *teach* them a lesson," I wonder what he thought
they would *learn*. In a war, a soldier is *less likely*
to die than a civilian. He looks *like* he hates our freedoms.
You don't know them *like* I do. He looks *as if* he hates
our freedoms. You don't know them *as* I do.
When in his sorrow my father said, "Everybody
loose in war," I knew exactly what he meant. It *may be*
poets should fight wars. *Maybe* then, metaphors—
not bodies, not hillsides, not hospitals, not schools—
will explode. I *might have* watched the popular sitcom
if not for my family—they were under attack,
they *might have* died. Others *may have* been laughing
at jokes while bodies were being torn apart.
I could not risk that kind of laughter. Of all the *media*

65

covering war, which *medium* best abolishes the truth?
I deceive *myself.* I will deceive you *myself.* In the Bronx,
I *passed* as Puerto Rican. I *passed* as Greek in Queens,
also Brazilian, Pakistani, Bangladeshi, even a famous,
good-looking American movie actor. As Iranian
in Manhattan. At the mall in New Jersey,
the sales clerk guessed Italian. Where Henry Ford
was born, my hometown, I always *pass* as Arab.
I may look like the men in the great paintings
of the Near East but their lives, their ways, I assure you,
are in the *past. Plus,* except in those paintings,
or at the movies, I never saw Arabs with multiple wives,
or who rode camels, lived in silk tents, drank from
desert wells; *moreover,* it's time to move *past* that.
Did language *precede* violence? Can violence *proceed*
without language? It broke my father's heart
to talk about the *principle* of equal justice.
The news aired several *quotations* from the airline
passengers, one of whom was a middle-aged man
with children, who said, "I didn't feel safe with them
on board." He used the word "them" though only one,
an Arab, was on the plane. Being from Detroit,
I couldn't help but think of Rosa Parks.
Then I got angry. I said to the TV, to no one
in particular, "If you don't feel safe, then you
get off the goddamn plane." You can *quote* me
on that. I was *really* angry—not *real* angry,
but *really* angry. The *reason?* A poet asked me
why I didn't write poems about Muslim and Arab
violence against others, and I said I did. And then
he said he meant violence against Americans and Israelis,
respectively, and I said I did, and before I could
go on he interrupted to ask why I didn't write
poems about mothers who sent their sons and daughters
on suicide missions. As if, as if, as if. I *respectfully*
decline to answer any more questions. Write your own
goddamn poem! Does this poem gratify the physical senses?
Does it use *sensuous* language? It certainly does not

attempt to gratify those senses associated with
sexual pleasure. In this way, it may not be a *sensual* poem.
However, men have been known to experience
sexual gratification in situations involving power,
especially over women, other men, life, and language.
My father said, "No matter how angry they make you,
invite the agents in the house, offer them coffee,
be polite. If they stay long, ask them to *sit*. Otherwise,
they will try to *set* you straight." When in his
frustration he said, "*Should of,* could of, would of,"
he meant, "Stop, leave me alone, I refuse to examine
the problem further." Because (not *since*) the terrorists
attacked us, we became more like the rest of the world
than ever before. This is *supposed* to be a poem;
it is *supposed* to be in a conversation with you.
Be *sure to* participate. "No language is more violent
than another," he said. *Then* he laughed, and said,
"Except the one you use." Do conflicts of interest
exist when governments award wartime contracts
to companies *that* have close ties to government officials?
From 1995 to 2000, Dick Cheney, Vice President
of the United States, was CEO of Halliburton,
which is headquartered in Houston, Texas,
near Bush International Airport. Would they benefit
themselves by declaring war? Please send *those* men
back home. My grandfather lay *there* unconscious.
For days, *there* was no water, no medicine, nothing
to eat. The soldiers left *their* footprints at the doorstep.
His sons and daughters, *they're* now grieving him.
"Try not *to* make *too* much of it" was the advice given
after *two* Homeland Security agents visited my house,
not once, not twice, but three times. I'm *waiting for*
my right mind. The language is a long *ways* from here.
After the bombs fell, I called every night to find out
whether my father was alive or dead. He always asked,
"How's the *weather* there?" Soon enough, he assured me,
things would return to normal, *that* (not *where*)
a ceasefire was on the way. *Although* (not *while*)

I spoke English with my father, he replied in Arabic.
Then I wondered, *who's* to decide *whose* language it is
anyway—you, me? *your* mother, father, books,
perspective, sky, earth, ground, dirt, dearly departed,
customs, energy, sadness, fear, spirit, poetry, God,
dog, cat, sister, brother, daughter, family, *you*, poems,
nights, thoughts, secrets, habits, lines, grievances,
breaks, memories, nightmares, mornings, faith, desire,
sex, funerals, metaphors, histories, names, tongues,
syntax, coffee, smoke, eyes, addiction, witness, paper,
fingers, skin, *you, your, you're* here, there, the sky,
the rain, the past, sleep, rest, live, stop, go, breathe

NOTES

"Being Muslim": *Ta' Ha', Ya Sin, Sad, Qaf*: The Qur'an contains suras with the preceding Arabic letters as their titles, which are thought to be mysterious, as what they stand for is not known.

"In a Perfect World": "There is a word for what he does, // a simple word, and the word / moves through the world, / and its melody is silence" is adapted from a sentence by Donald Justice in "The Man Closing Up," from *Night Light* and *New Selected Poems*. The lines by Justice are: "There is a word for it, / A simple word, / And the word goes around."

"In Memoriam": "America makes everything easy, except life" is attributed to poet and scholar Sharif Elmusa.

"Narrative": "so I just sat there. / then I saw the spider making a web/ across a window. / I found a match, walked over, / lit it and burned the spider to / death. / then I felt better. / much better" is excerpted from Charles Bukowski's "me against the world" in *Betting on the Muse*.

"O Mother, O Father": "You there, always and forever there, in the termination that obliterates everything else. O my mother" (re-lineated here) is from Hayden Carruth's "Mother" in *Tell Me Again How the White Heron Rises and Flies Across the Nacreous River at Twilight Toward the Distant Islands*.

"You": 1. the pronoun of the second person singular or plural, used of the person or persons being addressed. 2. (used nominatively as the subject of a sentence). 3. one; anyone; people in general. 4. (used in apposition with the subject of a sentence, sometimes repeated for emphasis following the subject). 5. (used by a writer or speaker in direct address). 6. (used rhetorically in addressing a person or persons not present or in personifying an object). 7. (used by a speaker or writer in referring to a particular profession, nationality, political party, etc). 8. (used in the predicate following a copulative verb). 9. (used as the direct object of a verb). 10. (used as the object of a preposition). 11. (used as an indirect object). 12. Informal. (used in place of the pronoun your with a gerund). 13. Archaic. yourself; yourselves. 14. the nature of character of the person addressed. 15. something or someone closely identified with or resembling the person addressed.